BUY NOW, PAY LATER

THOMPSON YARDLEY

BUY NOW, PAY LATER

THE MILLBROOK PRESS · BROOKFIELD, CONNECTICUT

Library of Congress Cataloging-in-Publication Data

Yardley, Thompson, 1951–
Buy now, pay later : smart shopping counts / by Thompson Yardley.
p.   cm.—(A Lighter look book)
Includes index.
Summary: Explains how being a smart shopper and a wise consumer can
help protect the environment and promote good health, covering such
topics as supermarket shopping, food production and processing, and
recycling.
ISBN 1-56294-149-6
1. Consumer education—Juvenile literature.   2. Ecology—Juvenile
literature. [1. Consumer education. 2. Ecology.] I. title.
II. Series.   3. Shopping.
TX335.5.Y37   1992
640'.73—dc20   91-22497   CIP   AC

First published in the United States in 1992 by
The Millbrook Press Inc.
2 Old New Milford Road
Brookfield, Connecticut 06804
© Copyright Cassell plc 1991
First published in Great Britain in 1991 by
Cassell Publishers Limited
5   4   3   2   1

DON'T BE A CARELESS SHOPPER!

Read this book first.
Careless shopping damages the world!
Let's follow an ordinary family on a
trip to a supermarket and find out . . .

how to save energy when you go shopping!

what to look for on package labels!

how to help wild animals and farm animals!

how hamburgers eat up forests!

What would you sell if you had a store?

LOTS OF GOODIES!?

ICE CREAM!

CANDY!

COMICS!

TOYS!

But people need other things too! For instance, what about . . .

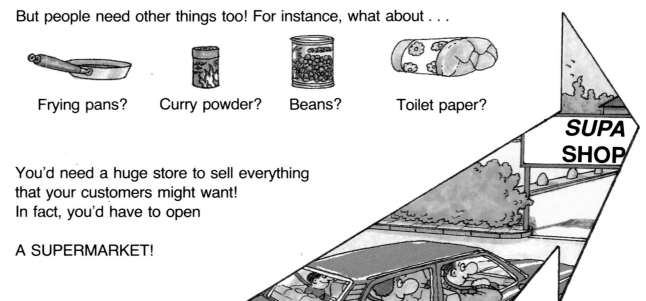

Frying pans?   Curry powder?   Beans?   Toilet paper?

You'd need a huge store to sell everything
that your customers might want!
In fact, you'd have to open

A SUPERMARKET!

SUPA
SHOP

WHAT DID YOU BUY THIS WEEK?

Lots of families do their shopping in a supermarket . . .

They usually take a shopping list like this . . .

SATURDAY ~ SUPERMARKET

Hamburger	Chicken
Bread	Potatoes
Paper Towels	Spaghetti
Hand Soap	2 Cans of Tuna
Toilet Cleaner	Pineapple
Lemonade	Corn
Fish Sticks	Dishwashing Liquid
Cans of Soda	Dog Food
Toothpaste	Corned Beef
Bananas	Cheese
Melon	Baked Beans
Eggs	Tea Bags

Most shoppers buy more things than they have on their shopping lists.

Find out how many things your family buys in a week.

CHECK OUT THE CHECKOUT!

Save up all those sales receipts and see how much your family spends.

WE BUY THINGS WE NEED

Everybody needs food and water, a home to live in, clothes to wear, and good health.

FOOD AND WATER
We need good food and water to be able to live and grow.

CLOTHES AND SHELTER
We need clothes to protect us from the weather. We need homes to shelter us, too.

HEALTH AND HYGIENE
We need to keep our bodies healthy to enjoy a happy life.

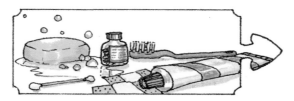

WE BUY THINGS WE LIKE

People get bored eating plain food, wearing dull clothes, and so on.
They like to have a bit of variety . . .

FUN FOOD AND DRINK
Ordinary food made from flour, such as bread, isn't nearly as much fun to eat as spaceship-shaped macaroni!

FASHION CLOTHES
It's fashionable to be seen wearing a T-shirt from the latest adventure movie.

BEAUTIFUL HOMES
People like to make their homes look nice and clean. They buy things such as blue disinfectant for their toilets.

We do about half of our shopping in supermarkets . . .

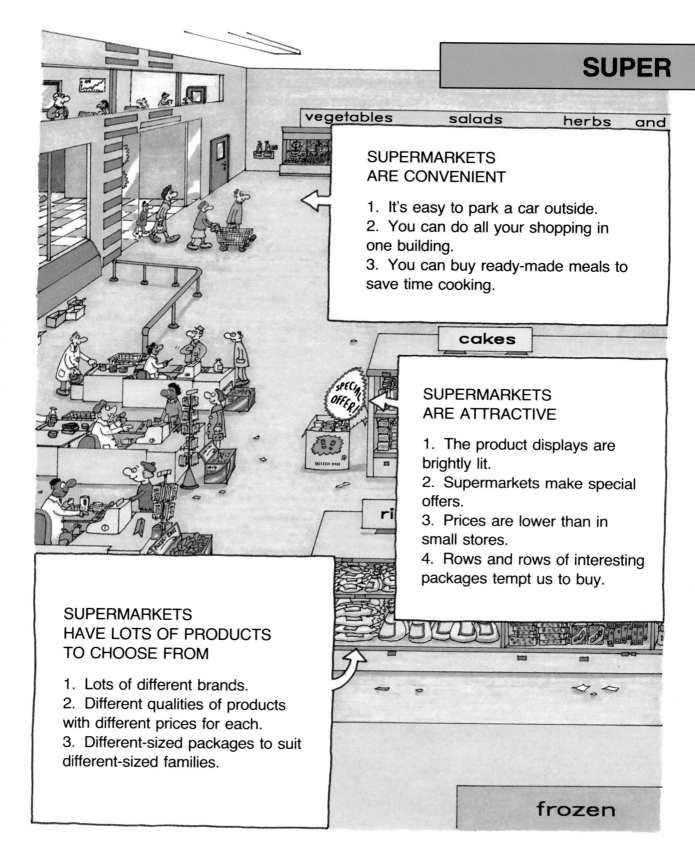

vegetables   salads   herbs   and

**SUPERMARKETS
ARE CONVENIENT**

1. It's easy to park a car outside.
2. You can do all your shopping in one building.
3. You can buy ready-made meals to save time cooking.

cakes

SPECIAL OFFER!

**SUPERMARKETS
ARE ATTRACTIVE**

1. The product displays are brightly lit.
2. Supermarkets make special offers.
3. Prices are lower than in small stores.
4. Rows and rows of interesting packages tempt us to buy.

**SUPERMARKETS
HAVE LOTS OF PRODUCTS
TO CHOOSE FROM**

1. Lots of different brands.
2. Different qualities of products with different prices for each.
3. Different-sized packages to suit different-sized families.

frozen

[10]

SUPERMARKETS

spices   fruit

fresh meat

SPECIAL OFFER!
ANIMAL
BALLOONS

ead

flour   corn

food

SUPERMARKET
SHELVES ARE USUALLY FULL

1. You can buy the same products all year-round.
2. Big supermarkets are often located in shopping malls, where there are many different types of stores. You can buy almost anything you can think of at a mall.

SUPERMARKETS
ARE USUALLY HYGIENIC

1. Almost everything in a supermarket is sealed in hygienic packaging.
2. Chilled food and food for the freezer is kept cold, so that it doesn't go bad too quickly.
3. Most packages have a "sell by" date on the label. If a product isn't bought by this date, the supermarket throws it away because it might have gone bad. Some supermarkets give their "out of date" products to charities.

JUNK FOOD

Supermarkets are usually hygienic. But that doesn't mean that everything they sell is good for you. What you buy is up to you!

All the displays are attractive. They can tempt us to buy the wrong sort of food. This sort of food is called junk food. We can't just live on cookies and candy. We need to eat green vegetables, fruits, and some animal products, too.

And people who eat too much sweet or fatty food can get very fat.

FAT FACT
Not all fat people eat too much. Some people put on weight just by eating normal amounts of food. People like this have to be very careful about what they eat.

Additives are chemicals that food scientists add to food. Additives are used to color food, to flavor food, and to preserve food. But some food makers also use additives to fool people. Did you know that there's no chocolate in some chocolate cakes?

Cake without coloring   Coloring additive   Fake chocolate cake

Some food makers add a brown chemical color to make their cakes look chocolatey!

OLD ADDITIVES FACT

Salt and vinegar have been used for thousands of years to preserve food.

Pickled onions   Salted fish

These two additives stop food from going bad.

And how about those nice pink sausages? Real meat sausages are almost gray. But a red color is added to make them look more tasty.

Food scientists could easily make pink chocolate cake or even green sausages!

Plain gray sausage   Add a red color   Tasty-looking sausage

BLERRGH!

Some chemical colors can give people zits.

ZZZZZ!

Other chemical colors can make people feel tired.

CAREFUL SHOPPING GUIDE

Some additives affect the health of sensitive people.

For example:

So . . .

1. Always try to buy fresh food.

2. Check out package labels. Avoid fake flavors and colors when you can.

ANIMALS AND CHEMICALS

In most countries, the law says that new additives have to be tested. This is to see if they're safe before they're used. Animals are almost always used for these tests.

ADDITIVES
A new food additive might be tried out on a pig. But it's not just additives that are tested on animals. For example . . .

COSMETICS
A new hair spray might be tried on mice.

MEDICINES
New medicines are tested on animals, too. Scientists first make the test animals ill by injecting them with germs. Then they give them the new medicine.

Some of these products turn out to be useful. But some are discovered to be deadly poisons!

ANIMALS AND YOU

DOES TESTING DO ANY GOOD?

Chemicals injure animals and human bodies in different ways. So testing new products on animals doesn't always mean that they're safe for people.

CAREFUL SHOPPING GUIDE

1. Stick to well-tried medicines and cosmetics.

2. If you have to use new products, check the labels. Some companies don't test their products on animals.

3. Sometimes there's no information on the label. The salesperson might not know much either. Write to the manufacturers to find out if their products have been tested on animals.

And remember to throw out old, unused medicines. Some medicines become poisonous after they've been stored for a long time.

Of course, most animals aren't used for experiments.

THEY'RE USED FOR FOOD!

OLD McDONALD'S FARM

"Here a quack, there a quack, everywhere a quack quack."

Everybody knows what a nursery-rhyme farm looks like. Pigs, horses, chickens, sheep, and cows all living together, having farmyard fun!

But these days, many farmers don't let their animals have any fun.
Animals are often confined and fed artificial food.
So . . . modern farms often look like prisons!

Farms like these are sometimes called factory farms.
They make all sorts of other animal products as well as meat.
Here are just a few of them . . .

Many people think it's wrong to keep animals in cages or sheds.

But factory farmers say that their animals are safer and happier indoors.

WHAT DO YOU THINK?

If you support old-fashioned farms, follow . . .

CAREFUL SHOPPING GUIDE

1. If you buy animal products, look at the labels. Some stores sell "free-range" products. This means that the animals haven't been kept in factory farms.

2. You don't need to eat meat all the time to stay healthy. Try to cut down meat-eating to once or twice a week. Vegetarians are people who don't eat meat at all.

MEAT AND WILDLIFE

Not all meat products come from factory farms.

And the supermarket doesn't have cows in a field around back!

CHOPPED-DOWN TREES FACT

In 1950 there were twice as many trees in the Earth's forests as there are now!

Some cattle and sheep are raised on huge open farms called RANCHES. Beef cattle need a lot of open space. Cattle ranchers in Brazil cut down thousands of trees each week to clear the way for new ranches. The wild animals that live in the trees lose their homes. So . . . buying too many hamburgers may damage wildlife!

SHOCKING SHEEP FACT

There are about 160 million sheep in Australia. That's ten times as many sheep as people!

TREES AND SOIL
Trees and grass also help stop soil from being blown or washed away. Some scientists think that the Sahara Desert was caused by sheep and goats that ate all the grass. Parts of Australia are running out of grassland too!

Much of the meat from ranches is made into pet food.

FISH STICKS AND FISH

Floating fish factory

Fish are one of the few sorts of wild animals that we still hunt for food.

They're caught in huge nets. Then floating factories turn them into fish fillets or fish sticks. If we catch too many fish, there won't be enough left to produce more fish.

CANNED FISH
Sometimes we buy our fish in cans. Canning stops the fish from going bad on its long trip to the supermarket. But making cans uses up valuable metals such as aluminum and steel. These metals are wasted when we throw away the empty containers.

FISH STICKS
Fish sticks are easier to cook than fresh fish. But long cold storage and additives make them lose some of their goodness.

CAREFUL SHOPPING GUIDE

1. Buy fresh fish whenever possible.

2. Eat fish that has been caught locally.

3. Don't be tempted by attractive packaging.

WHALE FOOD
Most countries have stopped hunting whales because they had almost died out. Some countries have started fishing for krill. These tiny shrimplike animals are food for some types of whales. So . . . if we catch too many krill, we'll still be killing whales!

Krill

Whale

FRUITS AND VEGETABLES

We don't just need meat products for food. We need fruits and vegetables, too. They contain chemicals that our bodies need.

Plants make these chemicals from the soil as well as the air and water. Then they pass the chemicals on to us when we eat them.

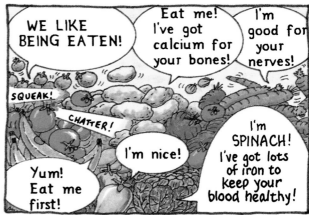

WE LIKE BEING EATEN!

Eat me! I've got calcium for your bones!

I'm good for your nerves!

SQUEAK!

CHATTER!

I'm nice!

Yum! Eat me first!

I'm SPINACH! I've got lots of iron to keep your blood healthy!

Growing too many crops can cause deserts to form.

All crops need soil to grow in and lots of water. The soil contains chemicals that the plants need too.

But some farmers grow more crops than is good for the land. These extra crops use up too much water and soil chemicals.

So . . . farmers have to add extra water and artificial chemicals to the soil. They also add chemicals to kill insects that might eat their crops. This poisons the soil and can injure other wildlife. These chemicals can soak into our drinking water!

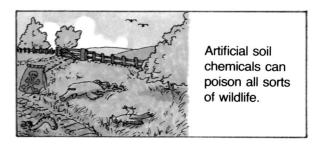

Artificial soil chemicals can poison all sorts of wildlife.

I wonder if bottled water is safe??

Bottled water is usually safe to drink.

BUYING ORGANIC

Farmers who don't use artificial chemicals are called organic farmers. They look after the soil by not growing too many plants.

And . . . organic crops are good for us. We need the right amounts of soil chemicals in the plants we eat in order to stay healthy.

CAREFUL SHOPPING GUIDE

1. Get your parents to buy organic food when they can. Look for labels at the store. Organic crops may cost a little more, but it's worth it to protect your health.

2. If you've got space for a garden, try growing your own crops!

Not all crops are used for food. For example . . . COTTON

INCREDIBLE SHRINKING SEA FACT

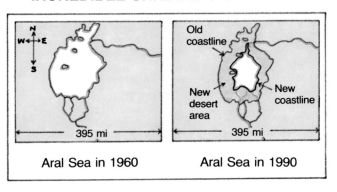

Aral Sea in 1960   Aral Sea in 1990

Cotton is a crop that needs an enormous amount of water to grow. If you buy any cotton clothes, look after them. They will have cost the world a lot of water to make.

The Aral Sea is in the USSR. Rivers that flow into it have been used to water huge cotton fields. This has caused the sea to shrink and turned its coastline into a desert!

DIGGING FOR TOOTHPASTE!

Of course, we don't just go shopping for food. We also buy nonfood items such as toothpaste, soap, teapots, and lawn mowers.

These sorts of things are made from raw materials dug from the ground.

Some people even dig for toothpaste!

HEY, LOOK! It's our dentist!

"TOOTHPASTE MINE" FACT

A mountain of waste like this is called a spoil heap.

TOOTHPASTE TOOTHBRUSH ~ AND CUP ~ SPECIAL OFFER!

Toothpaste is made of a fine white clay called china clay. Water and chemicals are added before it's packed into tubes. China clay is also used to make pottery.

We have to shift a lot of rock and soil to get at most raw materials. So after years of digging, ugly piles of waste build up.

But there isn't an endless supply of raw materials. Take coal, for example . . .

Looks like we're lost again, Bert!

COAL HOLE FACT
Coal is one of the raw materials used to make medicines, dyes, and clothes.

Some experts think we'll run out of coal in another two hundred years. Coal is getting hard to find even now!

OIL ABOARD!

You can buy automobile oil in many supermarkets. Lots of things, such as plastic, are made of oil too.

Oil is taken from the ground—from oil wells. Then it's shipped all over the world in huge tankers. And accidents will happen!

BUT THAT'S NOT ALL!

Factories must use energy to turn raw materials into products. Power stations supply this energy by burning coal, oil, or gas. These burning fuels pollute the air with millions of tons of waste gases. So the more products we buy or waste . . .

- The more raw materials we dig up!
- The more energy we use!
- The more we damage the environment!

OILY BIRDS AND FISH FACT

In 1989, the tanker *Exxon Valdez* ran aground in Alaska. Some 11 million gallons (40 million liters) of crude oil spilled into the sea.

CAREFUL SHOPPING GUIDE

You can help to solve these problems by careful shopping!

1. Buy longer-lasting products.

2. Don't waste them or misuse them.

3. Don't throw anything away before it's worn out.

WHAT'S PACKAGING FOR?

Most of the things on supermarket shelves are packed in boxes, bottles, jars, and cans. This packaging makes shopping easier for customers and storekeepers.

1. KEEPING STUFF IN
Most food products need some sort of packaging. Think what it would be like taking home loose jam!

2. PORTION CONTROL
Years ago, all food was sold loose. The storekeeper had to weigh the products and pack bags for each customer. Shopping is quicker these days. Carefully measured portions are prepackaged before they're sent to the stores. But that means you sometimes have to buy more than you need!

3. HYGIENE
Modern packaging helps to keep food fresh. Take corned beef, for example. When it is made, it's packed into cans. Then it's heated to kill off any bacteria it may contain. Cans of corned beef can be eaten after being stored for years!

AND WHAT'S IT MADE OF?

Just like everything else we buy, packaging is made from raw materials.

1. GLASS

Glass is made by mixing and heating limestone, soda, and sand. There are plenty of these raw materials. But it takes a lot of energy to turn them into glass. Some stores sell drinks in returnable glass bottles. These are refilled and used again and again and again. So returnable bottles save energy!

2. PLASTIC

Most plastics are made from oil. Some scientists say we'll run out of oil by the year 2020. The more plastic we buy and throw away, the sooner we'll run out of oil!

3. METAL

Cans are made of steel or aluminum. Two million tons of aluminum are used every year for packaging!

SO... how many of these would that make?

An average tree makes 14 tons of waste paper.

4. PAPER AND CARDBOARD

Take a look in your garbage can. Most of your trash is paper and cardboard packaging. Much of this is made of wood from trees!

LOADSATRASH!

Some manufacturers get completely carried away with their packaging!

HOW ABOUT A NICE CUP OF TEA?

Tea leaves

Tea leaves packed into a dunking bag

Tea leaves in a dunking bag with a fancy stapled label

Individual sachet for dunking bag of tea leaves with a fancy stapled label

Box for twenty-four individual sachets of dunking bags of tea leaves with fancy stapled labels

Free foldout guide to making the best tea, with fancy stapled labels in twenty-four individual sachets

and plastic wrapping around all of it!

When shoppers buy products, they have to buy the packaging too. Half the cost of some products is just for the packaging!

Not only do we pay for the packaging, we pay to get rid of it too.

Trash is either dumped or burned. Dumping uses up valuable land and pollutes the soil and the sea. Burning trash pollutes the air.

Some stores sell loose products such as herbs, coffee, candy, and tea in paper bags. These bags are cheap and can be used again.

ERK!

TO THE SIMPLE PACKAGING STORE

TRY THIS TONGUE TWISTER

PRETTY PACKAGES POSE PROBLEMS, PUMP UP PRICES, AND PRODUCE POLLUTION!

environmentally friendly dishwashing liquid

Look for biodegradable shopping bags!

LESS RUBBISH!

Some of the trash we dump rots away in the ground. Bacteria in the soil break it down by eating it. But most plastics don't rot away because bacteria can't eat them. When a product or its packaging can be eaten by bacteria, it's called biodegradable. Look for products or containers labeled biodegradable.

We waste our money and the world's raw materials by throwing old packaging away. But we can use some containers over again. This is called recycling. Find out how to cut down on waste by recycling. You can recycle . . .

- glass bottles and jars
- paper and cardboard
- metal cans
- some plastic containers
- and lots more!

RUSSIAN PACKAGE FACT
At the *GOM* supermarket in Moscow, products aren't always packaged. Shoppers can buy packaging at another store.

УПАКОВКА МАГАЗИН

CAREFUL SHOPPING GUIDE

1. Buy returnable bottles and cans. Try to avoid plastic containers.

2. Go for simple, cheap packaging.

3. Look for biodegradable products and packaging.

MUNCH!! SLURP!! YUM YUM! HUNGRY BACTERIA

4. Find out which local stores will let you bring your own containers.

5. Try to find several different ways to recycle used packaging.

BEANS

HOW TO PLAY

1. You need a drawing of a shopping cart on a small piece of index card for each player.

2. Use a dice. Each player rolls the dice in turn. The first to roll a six starts the game.

3. Follow the rules written on the squares. The first player to get to the exit is the winner.

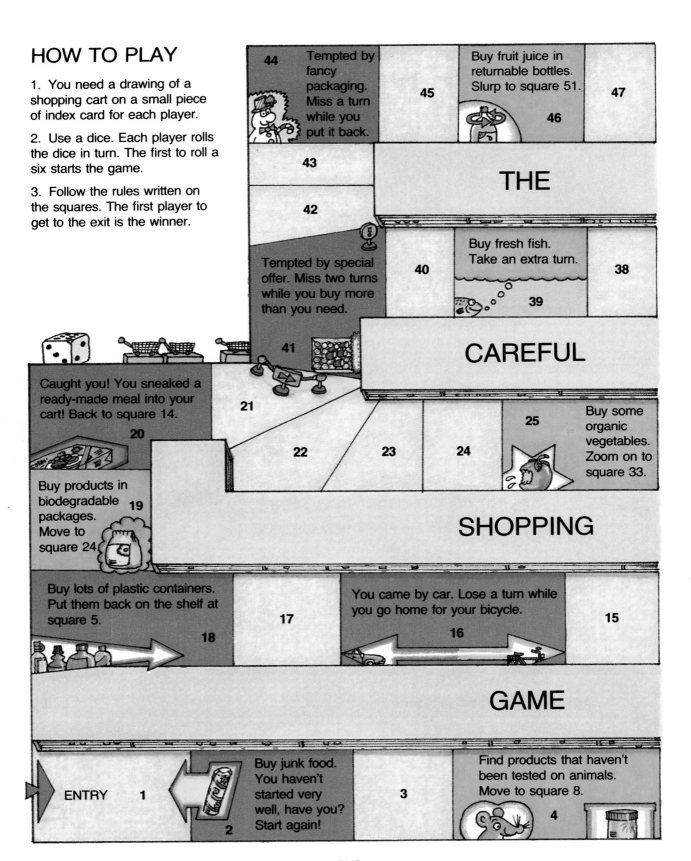

44 Tempted by fancy packaging. Miss a turn while you put it back.

45

Buy fruit juice in returnable bottles. Slurp to square 51.

46

47

43

42

THE

Tempted by special offer. Miss two turns while you buy more than you need.

40

Buy fresh fish. Take an extra turn.

39

38

41

CAREFUL

Caught you! You sneaked a ready-made meal into your cart! Back to square 14.

20

21

22

23

24

25

Buy some organic vegetables. Zoom on to square 33.

Buy products in biodegradable packages. Move to square 24.

19

SHOPPING

Buy lots of plastic containers. Put them back on the shelf at square 5.

18

17

You came by car. Lose a turn while you go home for your bicycle.

16

15

GAME

ENTRY   **1**

Buy junk food. You haven't started very well, have you? Start again!

2

3

Find products that haven't been tested on animals. Move to square 8.

4

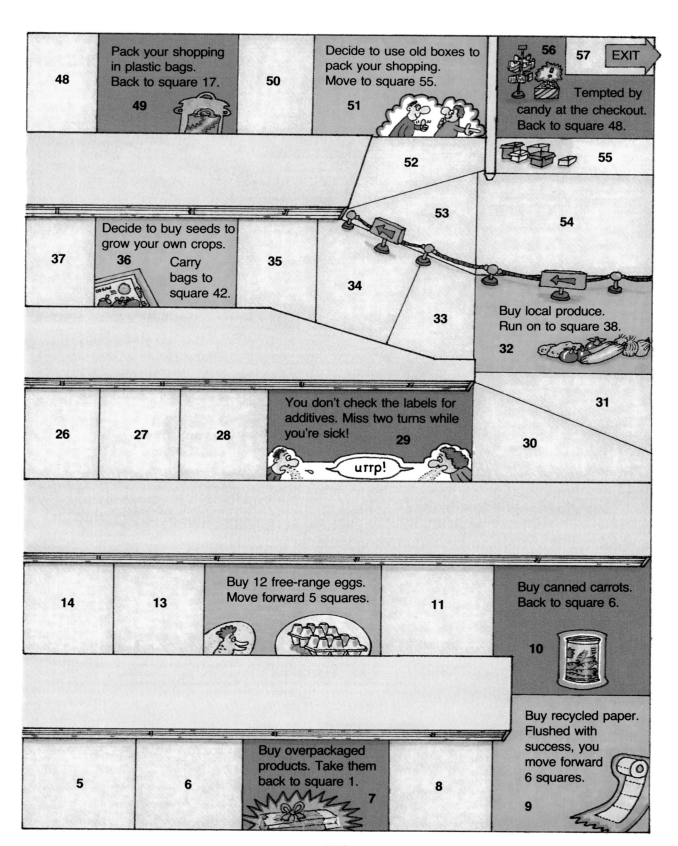

ON THE ROAD

Most big supermarkets are built outside towns. They're designed for people with cars. People without cars have to manage as best they can.

The more we use cars for shopping, the more fuel we use and the more pollution there is!

All the items we buy in supermarkets are brought by trucks or vans. There are about 100 million delivery vehicles on the world's roads. They all use gas or diesel fuel and give off smoky waste gases.

OFF THE ROAD

Airplanes and ships bring products from around the world. Many of these could be produced locally.

Needlessly transporting stuff from thousands of miles away is a waste of fuel and raw materials!

CAREFUL SHOPPING GUIDE

1. Do your shopping close to where you live. Using local stores helps them stay in business. Local stores are better for poor, disabled, or old people who might not have a car.

2. Don't go shopping by car if you don't need to. Use public transportation, or walk or bicycle to the stores.

3. Look at the labels on products. Try to buy things that have been made or grown as locally as possible.

Nowadays we eat and use products from all over the world
without thinking much about it.

Find out about THE AMAZING WORLD OF DINNERS! See if you can do the

COOK'S TOUR QUIZ!

Each of the items in this dining room comes from different
countries. Can you find the countries on the map?

Pineapple—Philippines

Wheat bread—Canada

Corn—United States

Spaghetti—Italy

Tuna fish—Fiji

Melon—Paraguay

TV—Japan

Potatoes—Egypt

Bananas—Suriname

Plates—Taiwan

Baked beans—Mexico

TV show—Australia

Dog food (beef)—Argentina
Dog food (soybean meal)—China

Tablecloth—Ireland

Cheese—Netherlands

Corned beef—Kenya

Glasses—Denmark

Chairs—Brazil

Place mats—Sri Lanka

Cutlery—South Korea

ANSWERS TO COOK'S TOUR QUIZ:

1. Egypt
2. Italy
3. Fiji
4. Paraguay
5. Suriname
6. Canada
7. Philippines
8. United States
9. Mexico
10. Netherlands
11. Kenya
12. Argentina
13. China
14. Taiwan
15. Sri Lanka
16. Brazil
17. Denmark
18. Japan
19. Australia
20. Ireland
21. South Korea

AFTER-DINNER HINTS

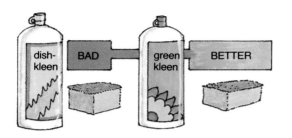

WASHING DISHES
Old-fashioned dishwashing liquids aren't always biodegradable. Some new types are. But . . . they still come in plastic containers, so they waste raw materials. Recycle the container!

CLEANING UP
Some people have more than one garbage can. But they're not being greedy—they're being careful! Why not try to split up your trash like this?

COMPOST BIN	METAL BIN	GLASS BIN	PAPER BIN	PLASTICS BIN
For vegetable scraps. These can be saved in the bin until bacteria have biodegraded them. This produces compost that can be spread on the garden to help plants grow.	For bottle tops, cans, and so on. These can be taken to your recycling center.	For bottles and jars. Most of these aren't returnable. But you can save them for recycling.	For clean paper and cardboard, which can be taken to your local recycling center.	For plastic items. Many things made of plastic, including milk and soda bottles, can be recycled.

LITTER LITTER LITTER LITTER LITTER LITTER

SOME CARELESS PEOPLE USE THE STREETS AS GARBAGE CANS

Have you ever thrown a candy wrapper on the ground? It's not really litter is it? It's only a small piece of paper or plastic. But what would happen if everybody thought like that?
If we all put our trash in the streets and parks, the world would look like this!

FOOTBALL LITTER FACT

At a big football game, the crowd may drop as much as 20 tons of litter in the stadium!

LEAF LITTER
Sweeping streets and parks costs a lot of money. But if everybody looked after the environment, we would only need to sweep up fallen leaves.

LITTER OF THE LAW
Litter could be expensive for you too. In most countries, you can be fined for littering.

And litter can be dangerous!

A DANGEROUS NEWSPAPER

A DANGEROUS BOTTLE

DANGEROUS BUBBLE GUM
(AMONG OTHER THINGS!)

CAREFUL LITTER GUIDE

You can help to keep our planet clean and tidy.

1. Most litter is found near stores. Ask the owner of your local store to put a litter bin outside the store.

2. Get your teacher to organize litter pick-up squads at your school!

Careless shopping ruins the world for everybody.
Now that you've read this book, you know that careful shopping
helps to keep our planet safe and healthy.

BUY LESS NOW
AND SAVE THE WORLD LATER!

FIND OUT MORE

Now that you know how to be a smart shopper, you may want to learn more about helping the Earth through choosing products wisely and using them responsibly. Here are some books to look for in the library:

50 Simple Things Kids Can Do To Save the Earth, by the Earth Works Group (Andrews and McMeel, 1990)

How on Earth Do We Recycle Glass?, by Joanna Randolph Rott and Seli Groves (Millbrook, 1992)

How on Earth Do We Recycle Metal?, by Rudi Kouhoupt with Donald B. Marti (Millbrook, 1992)

How on Earth Do We Recycle Paper?, by Helen Jill Fletcher and Seli Groves (Millbrook, 1992)

How on Earth Do We Recycle Plastic?, by Janet Potter d'Amato with Laura Stephenson Carter (Millbrook, 1992)

A Kid's Guide to How to Save the Planet, by Billy Goodman (Avon, 1990)

INDEX